Digger's

Andy Graves

BookLeaf Publishing

Digger's Ditties © 2022 Andy Graves

All rights reserved.

No part of this publication may be reproduced, stored in a retrieval system, or transmitted, in any form or by any means, electronic, mechanical, photocopying, recording or otherwise, without the prior written permission of the presenters.

Andy Graves asserts the moral right to be identified as author of this work.

Presentation by *BookLeaf Publishing*

Web: www.bookleafpub.com

E-mail: info@bookleafpub.com

ISBN: 9789357617048

First edition 2022

To Kate

ACKNOWLEDGEMENT

Kate my wife for her forensic proof reading
To all the members of the South Central
Ambulance Service that I worked with over 30
plus years. Especially to those still answering
and responding to the never ending calls
And to all those who have encouraged me to
publish my work for many years

PREFACE

This is a collection of poems I have written over recent years.

Some from my time as a paramedic others inspired by childhood recollections or things and events going on around me

Poetic Licence

Poetry affects you differently to prose,
As rhythm and meter ebbs and flows.

It can touch your heart, less made of stone,
Or hit you squarely in the funny bone.

Grammar can go - take a hike,
Things can be writ - anyway you like.

My style is usually quite simplistic,
I make no claims to skills linguistic.

I would like to write the odd haiku,
It's just a format I can't do!

Never tempted, a sonnet to try,
Shakespeare set standards too high.

Iambic pentameter or a Cinquain,
Really are too much of a strain.

I try to be relevant, occasionally profound,
As I comment upon the world around.

But it wouldn't be a Digger's Ditty,
If it wasn't just a little bit witty

So join with me as I explore
If I can write or am just a bore

These are my poems for good or bad
If you enjoy them then I'm glad

But if you feel it's all a conceit
Then I trust you kept the receipt

Situational Awareness

Our vehicle, a shade of yellow luminescence,
Strobing blue lights, request acquiescence.

The sirens issue their acoustic screech,
Grant us passage-they beseech.

Despite this assemblage of sight and sound,
Some drivers' actions, still confound!

We then have to try and deduct,
If they will stop or route obstruct,

On the crest of a hill or blind curve,
Putting a strain upon one's nerve.

*

Cars pull in, on carriageway dual,
But on single lane, that's not the rule,

When we follow a line of three,
The first in line, our lights will see,

They will pull in, to allow a pass,
But it is not so outlandish to forecast,

That 2nd in line will make mistake,
Of not checking mirrors before overtake!

*

On coming traffic may block our route,
As we travel to calls; often acute!

So the odd profanity, we may express,
If you impede our urgent progress!

Our contempt we don't try to disguise,
So best you don't try to meet our eyes!

Now we're not trained in Fortune Telling,
So if down the road you see us propelling,

Try just as quick as you can,
To make a space for the big yellow van.

The Colon

The Colon is not sexy,
the Colon is not cool,
But without one,
It's hard to pass a stool.

The Colon is not sexy,
The Colon is not chic,
But without one,
You're really up the creek.

The Colon is not sexy,
The Colon has no style,
But do give it a thought,
Every once in a while.

The Colon is not sexy,
It lacks imagination
It just does its job,
If not that's constipation!

Childhood memories

When I was young there was Watch with Mother
And other shows, watched with my brother

Pogles' Wood with Pippin and Tog,
The Herb Garden had Dill the Dog.

Trumpton ended by the band stand,
Fingerbobs had Yoffy, to give them a hand.

Andy Pandy and Looby Loo,
Chigley was near Trumpton too!

The Clangers lived on a dustbin lid moon,
The Soup dragon, had a very large spoon.

The Magic Roundabout with Dougal the dog,
I've nothing to say about Noggin the Nog!

Ivor the Engine with Jones the Steam,
The Wombles were a tidying team.

A musical Box for Camberwick Green,
Rhubarb and Custard, wobbled on screen.

Emily's Bagpuss always went to sleep,
Crystal Tipps and Alistair, never a peep!

Tales of the Riverbank, view from a bridge,
Then there was Mary, Mungo and Midge.

Mr Benn always dressed just right,
The Woodentops were in black and white.

My Flower Pot men had strings you could see,
Captain Pugwash was all at sea.

You may remember some, a few or all,
But these are my memories, of when I was
small.

Poetic License 2

Finding it hard tonight,
For something new to write.

Searching for a theme,
But as yet not a gleam.

Searching the news,
Looking for my muse.

But still, I am bereft,
May resort to theft.

Of great poetic feats,
Like something from Keats.

Or wait until it's dark,
To poach from Muriel Spark.

Would Milton really object,
If I stole from Bertolt Brecht?

Kipling, I could accost,
Or even, Robert Frost.

From Byron, I could pinch,
Larkin, is a cinch!

From Sassoon, I could swipe,
He's not around to gripe.

But for me to plagiarise,
Would not be very wise.

Word Power

Don't explain, expound
Don't suggest, propound

Don't leave, egress
Don't correct, redress

Don't whine, be querulous
Don't chat, be garrulous

Don't take part, contest
Don't use tact, finesse

Don't add, augment
Don't divide, segment

Don't just form, extrude
Don't stick out, protrude

Don't scatter, dissipate
Don't speak, articulate

Dawning on me

The horizon is lightening
The dawn drawing near
The birds morning symphony
Is all I can hear

Away in the distance
Trees stand silhouette
Against a paling background
Soft hues against the jet

Through peach to coral
Shades of aquamarine
Turquoise to teal
The pallet of this scene

Falling

Summer consigned to memory
The equinox has passed
Autumn now is with us
As the trees begin to cast

Leaves are on the change
Alterations to their tone
The gold and rusty tinges
Upon the ground lay prone

Like a whispering carpet
That every child has kicked
Jams and chutneys made
Fruit and berries picked

Visitors heading south
Migratory flights begin
We'll not see their kind again
Till long after spring

Harvest reaches completion
All safely baled and stored
Fields by the plowshare
Like corduroy are scored

The evenings drawing in
The sun lower in the sky
The passing of the seasons
Winter now is nigh

Digger's Decent

'Twas a cold and frosty morn
When tale of cycling woe was born

While peddling upon dark tow path
Not noting, low bridge to pass

Swerving to avoid impact fate
Descended into watery state

Arising from Grand Union depths
Extraction urgent, need to take steps

Pulling on, slippery bank
Sliding back, his heart sank

Calling on his guile and wit
Grabbed his bike and stood on it

Escaped at last from watery grave
Alas glasses, could not save

Staggering wet to MK base
Night crew met him face to face

Dripping wet from head to toe
Back to home, chose to go

Poor wife is dragged from her bed
We'll not repeat what she said

It's many years since this took place
But fade from memory is not the case

'Cos any mention of watery event
Requires retelling of Digger's decent

Sylvanian

Ubiquitous timber,
From singular sentinel,
To arboreal harbour.
Verdant companion,
The billboard of nature.

Provider of breath.
Dendritic sculptures,
Sweeping the sky,
Securing the earth.
Timeless yet transient,

These masts of nation,
The keel of our land.
From orchard to copse
Spinney and grove,
Remain, ever changing.

Tooth Decay

Bit the top off Walnut Whip,
Liquorish stick in Sherbet dip.

Never got near a Milk Tray,
Gobstoppers took nearly all day.

A Texan was a mighty chew,
A Curlywurly was still new.

Opal Fruits were rearranged.
Marathon had its name changed,

Black Jacks and Fruit Salad,
Just half a p (when it was valid).

Jelly Babies n Dolly Mixtures,
We're all, regular fixtures.

Love Hearts and Refreshers,
Were my childhood pleasures.

Not so much all the drilling,
And the ugly amalgam filling.

That it's almost beyond belief,
I've still got, my own teeth!

A void

This is a poem 'bout nothing!
It's just a hole in the air.
Hold it up to the light,
And it's like its not there.

It has no subject matter,
In fact no matter at all.
If you follow quantum theory,
It'd pass right through a wall.

I'd stop reading it now,
It's a total waste if time.
With no redeeming feature,
It's just an excuse of a rhyme.

PIN Pain

I have too many PINS,
That four digit code.
That I really do think,
My brain will explode!

One for the debit card,
Another for the phone.
Try to keep them different,
But to confusion I am prone.

Make them individual,
For each card or device!
Do not write them down,
That's the security advice.

Do not use your birthday,
Somebody might guess.
Nor you anniversary,
This is causing such distress.

And now I must confront,
The chip and pin machine.
Type in the numbers,
But keep the keys unseen.

How hard can it be?
Four numbers to recall.
I think I've got it sorted,
Then my hand begins to stall.

I do know the numbers,
Oh no! I've made a hash!
Oh! just forget it!
I'll pay for it in cash

Antithetical Contradictions

New nostalgia
Old revelations
Future memories
Past expectations

Public anonymity
Private exposure
Enigmatic simplicity
Open enclosure

Voluble reticence
Cleanly pollute
Obtuse transparency
Verbosely mute

Politely rude
Chance intention
Welcome torment
Liberated detention

Punctually tardy
Erratically consistent
Precisely careless
Nearly distant

Angrily sanguine
Idly engaged
Warily relaxed
Calmly enraged

Original copy
Factual illusion
Passive activity
Incipient conclusion

Adam's Ale

You chosen to imbibe,
As Friday night is here.
What do you prescribe?
The wine or the beer?

Something to facilitate,
Inhibitions to repress.
Something to inebriate,
Helping to de-stress.

Now your glass is empty again!
How about a wee dram?
But don't mix grape and grain
Or your brain cells get a slam!

English now a foreign tongue,
As the Shots they deliver,
Everything now must be sung,
Send a warning to the liver!

Then your words start to slur,
Risk assessment now impaired.
Memories begin to blur,
Saying things you've never dared.

Don't finish in hospital ward,
Or slumped on toilet floor.
Seeking help from The Lord,
As you recall the night before.

It's ok to have a drink,
In fact, as I recline,
I will join you, I think
In a glass or two of wine.

But if not prone to moderation,
As you really oughta!
Then you'll find true salvation,
In a glass or two of water.

The First Day (of the Somme)

O Seven Thirty, July the first
From thin lips, tightly pursed

Whistles trigger coldest sweat
Tommies emerge over parapet.

Explosions echo within the skull
Skylarks singing during brief lull

Stepping out 'cross cratered land
After barrage carefully planned

But Hun defences barely grazed
And by firing, ranks are razed.

New Battalions, quickly thinned
A cloud of khaki, dispersed by wind

Losses from Empire and British Isles
Progress comes in yards not miles.

Steadfast, showing greatest mettle
Thousand lost, once dust did settle

On that bright July morn
Pals from youth, abruptly shorn.

                            *

Conceived to relieve, Verdun pressure
Simply transposed that bloody thresher

Four months more the battles raged
Staggering losses, however gauged.

From Beaumont-Hamel to Delville Wood
Cemeteries now, where once men stood

Lines of headstones, crosses and stars
In silent testament to theirs and ours.

At Thiepval, so many listed
Of the thousands who enlisted

Their remains not yet found
Resting still, 'neath chalky ground.

They'll not weary nor grow old
As names yearly, are extolled

A century on, we still recall
Those who served and gave their all.

Stepping Off (D-day)

Overnight arrived on gossamer thread,
At dawn on Franco beaches tread.

Omaha, Utah. Sword, Juno and Gold,
Troops landed in venture, uncertain but bold.

From Pegasus Bridge to Sainte-Mère-Église,
As the coast of Europe they try to seize.

In tiny X-craft to ships of battle,
All too aware of the deathly rattle.

From Merville Battery and Pointe du Hoc,
They learn the reality of battle shock.

Despite resistance, a foothold gained,
Progress marked by beaches, stained.

Some still recall that momentous day,
This 75th anniversary of D-Day.

So spare a moment to reflect,
On those who stood tall and erect.

Crossed sea and sand, so hostile,
To fight a tyranny, cruel and vile.

For many was, the end of days,
And to them all, a glass I raise.

Tea

It can perk you up
or calm you down
Supped in the county
Or drunk around town

Will soften any biscuit
Delicious with toast
Sitting up a mountain
Or by the coast

Milk can be added
Can have it black
Late in the night
Or at dawn's crack

Brewed in the pot
Or straight from the bag
When feeling strained
Or you start to sag

Special in china
Great in a mug
The liquid version
Of a group hug

Forward Pass

Forwards
Backs

Run
Pass

Ruck
Maul

Scrum
Down

Line out
Put in

Brought down
Held up

Stand Off
Knock on

Tight head
Full back

Penalty
Try

Gain line
Contact

Drop goal
Conversion

Tackle hard
Soft hands

Loose head
Blind side

Hooker
Flanker

Off his feet
Side Step

Crash tackle
Hand off

Garry Owen
Twenty Two

Against the head
Cleared out

Collapse
Prop

Scrum Half
Full Back

Pride
Passion

Eighty minutes
In the bar

Compete
Respect

Rugby
Union

That's All Folks

Bugs Bunny, Daffy Duck,
Wile E Coyote had no luck.

Elmer Fudd, Yosemite Sam,
Always such an angry man.

Porky Pig said "That's all"
Road Runner, fastest of all?

Tom and Jerry always fighting,
Speedy Gonzales moved like lightning.

Stop the Pigeon, Wacky Races,
Hong Kong Phooey, solving cases.

Penelope Pitstop, The Hooded Claw.
The Anthill Mob came to the fore.

Yogi Bear with Boo Boo,
Shaggy and Scooby Doo.

Deputy Dawg and Muskrat,
Lots of things going splat!

Cartoon shorts from our past,
Seldom equaled, never surpassed!

Ingram Content Group UK Ltd.
Milton Keynes UK
UKHW050731240423
420680UK00016B/863

9 789357 617048